Discipleship Series

I0162780

The Great Possession

You have a possession that can earn you eternal life!

Bola Olu-Jordan

THE GREAT POSSESSION
You have a possession that can earn you eternal life!

Published by CRYOUT Publications
Africa. Miami. Edmonton

www.cryoutreach.com

Printed in the United States of America

DEDICATION

To Christ's followers in spirit and in truth.

CONTENTS

FOREWORD

While many rich people like Nicodemus and Joseph of Arimathaea were 'secret disciples' of Jesus, often using the cover of the night to visit, for fear of being identified with a man regarded as a religious bigot, a very rich and wealthy young man came running to him in the open, disregarding his wealth and social status, desperate to know what he could do to get to heaven and how he could use his wealth to earn himself eternal life.

Jesus, perhaps, knowing how difficult it is for young people to obey the law, let alone a young, wealthy man and a ruler at that, wanted to just *get the monkey off his back*, asked him to go keep the laws and he would be fine. But he was shocked when the man replied that he had been keeping not just part of the laws, but all from his youth.

Jesus gave him a second and closer look, a spiritual scanning sort of, to determine if that claim was really true and if the man was sincere enough. It was true. Then, Jesus "loved him". He discovered that only one thing was missing in his life, only one thing and if he could fix it, he would just be 'perfect'. But he couldn't.

If Jesus were to 'scan' you to determine what is missing in your life to qualify you for eternal life, how many things would He discover? That is the great possession you need to discover in your life and trade for eternal life. This book will show you how!

1
THE ETERNAL QUEST

*"Jesus looked round about, and saith unto his disciples,
How hardly shall they that have riches enter into the
kingdom of God! And the disciples were astonished at his
words" (*Mar. 10:23-24).

I n the Gospels, Jesus showed a very rich
and wealthy man who came desperately
running after Him, calling Him 'good
master' and desiring to know what he could do
to get to heaven how he could use his wealth to
earn himself eternal life.

At first, "Jesus said unto him, Why callest
thou me good? *there is* none good but one, *that is,*
God. Thou knowest the commandments, Do
not commit adultery, Do not kill, Do not steal,
Do not bear false witness, Defraud not, Honour
thy father and mother. And he answered and
said unto him, Master, all these have I observed
from my youth" (Mark 10:19).

Jesus knew how difficult it was for a young
man to obey the law, let alone a young, wealthy

man and a ruler. So, when he told Jesus that he had been keeping not just a part, but all the laws from his youth, it was like some of the encounters of Jesus where He had exclaimed that He never found such faith in Israel (Mat.8:10; Luke7:9). This was another surprising testimony from a very unlikely man and Jesus had to give him a second and closer look; perhaps a spiritual scanning, to determine if that claim was really true. Indeed, it was!

We must acknowledge the fact that for a man in such a position to love the Lord to the extent of risking and disregarding his social status and running after a man the religious, political and the aristocrats of the society deemed to be an outcast and a bigot, he must have gotten the true revelation of who Jesus was!

There were many of his caliber who preferred to come to Jesus in the cover of the night so that they would not be seen in the public, choosing to rather preserve their social or religious status than risk being associated with such a man like Jesus. Nicodemus and Joseph of Arimathaea were prominent among them (John 3:1-5; John 19:38), and many others who were called 'secret disciples' of Jesus. But this man disregarded all that and came boldly to Jesus in the open, sincerely asking Him about an important matter bordering on his eternity.

Jesus' initial response was more of *getting the monkey off his back*; something like 'why bother me about the major, when you are not willing to do the minor', sort of. But He was surprised at the man's reply when he said: Master, all these have I observed from my youth" (Mark 10:19).

This was an emphatic statement without the colouring of pride but of someone who want a way forward. Jesus gave him a second look, this time, to scan him to see if the man's claim was actually true. How could a young man in such a social position and financial status possibly keep not just a part of the law, but ALL! But Jesus discovered that it was not a bogus claim but a true one; "then Jesus beholding him loved him".

So, did this man actually possess what he needed to make eternal life? Jesus must have looked at him long enough to see through him life, to see if there was anything else needed for this man since he had passed the initial test. Jesus found out something and He said to him: "one thing thou lackest: go thy way, sell whatsoever thou hast, and give to the poor, and thou shalt have treasure in heaven: and come, take up the cross, and follow me" (10vs21).

It is interesting to know that just only one thing remained for the man to make heaven – just one thing! I wonder if Jesus have to look at us as He looked at the man and scan us in order to determine what remained in our lives to qualify for eternal life, I am afraid of how many things He would discover! No wonder Jesus loved the man. Would He love us in regards to our obeying Him? (Gal.2:16).

The fact is that law cannot and does not save, if it could, the man was a candidate of heaven already, because he had fulfilled all the laws from his youth and Jesus did not dispute that, but rather loved him. But when we get to the peak of the law, there is always something left, because "by the deeds of the law there shall no flesh be justified in his sight: for by the law *is* the knowledge of sin... Therefore we conclude that a man is justified by faith without the deeds of the law" (Rom.3:20,28). What is remaining at the end of the law is Jesus, for Jesus is the end of the law! (Rom.10:4).

Although, the man still recognized who Jesus was, but it is not in knowing Jesus, it is in following and obeying Him (Rom.2:13; James 1:22). When Jesus told him the one thing needed in his life and what to do with that one thing: the man "was sad at that saying, and went away grieved: for he had great possessions" (Mark 10:19-22).

2
LIFE APPLICATION

"For if they do these things in a green tree, what shall be done in the dry"? (Luk.23:31).

The story is a life application every believer must apply to his or her life as a spiritual self-examination so as to determine what great possessions we have that are too great or precious to us and we are unwilling to lay down to follow Jesus.

Although, the man had the commendation of the law, but Jesus is the only requirement to get to heaven, not the law, "by the deeds of the law there shall no flesh be justified in his sight". He is the way, the truth and the life. He said "I am the way, the truth, and the life: no man cometh unto the Father, but by me" (John 14:6). He is the door that leads to God. "I am the door of the sheep... I am the door: by me if any man enter in, he shall be saved, and shall go in and out, and find pasture" (John 10:7,9). The "one thing" he lacked was his comfort boat he was not willing to step out from.

Although, we are believers, attend church, have membership card, partake in ordinances, work in the church, love Jesus and the brethren and we even labour in ministry, which are wonderful things to do, but the only thing Jesus asks from us is perhaps the only possession difficult for us to let go in our lives. You must find out that one thing, or more in your life.

The young ruler abandoned Jesus and there was no record that he ever returned to Him. He gave up his desire to make heaven because he couldn't meet up the requirement to follow Jesus. (He was probably looking forward to some more stringent laws and doctrines he could keep, just like many today are keeping denominational doctrines which give them religious satisfaction). There is always something we posses that Jesus would take from us before we can follow Him. Our willingness to let go determines our readiness let God.

This man's pedigree was one of the finest in the Bible, but his end was a tragedy. He was looking for something to do, instead of someone to follow. Creeds, dogmas, laws, doctrines, etc are good giving a sense of performance, but obedience is what matters to God. "Hath the LORD *as great* delight in burnt offerings and sacrifices, as in obeying the voice of the LORD? Behold, to obey *is* better than sacrifice, *and* to hearken than the fat of rams." (1Sam.15:22).

3
RICHES AND CHRISTIAN

"But they that will be rich fall into temptation and a snare, and into many foolish and hurtful lusts, which drown men in destruction and perdition. For the love of money is the root of all evil: which while some coveted after, they have erred from the faith," (1Tim.6:9-10).

To this young ruler, although he loved the Lord, but his wealth was the snare which drowned him in destruction and eternal perdition. The Preacher says money is a defense (Eccl.7:12), but what happens when the defense is removed - and God will go after whatever is your defense, your trust, because He wants to be the only one occupying that place in your life. David said, "But the LORD is my defense; and my God *is* the rock of my refuge" (Psa. 94:22).

What are your own riches, wealth and possession that are too great for you to give up for eternal life? It may not be money, property or material thing, but there is definitely something you posses: perhaps, habit, friendship, views, vice, belief, etc, which one is yours? Perhaps, it is anger, malice, unforgiveness, bitterness, pride, jealousy, hatred, fault-finding, rebellion, etc. They are your possession and hindrance to the kingdom!

"And the disciples were amazed at his words. But Jesus answereth again, and saith unto them, Children, how hard is it for them that trust in riches to enter into the kingdom of God! It is easier for a camel to go through a needle's eye, than for a rich man to enter into the kingdom of God. And they were astonished out of measure, saying among themselves, Who then can be saved?" (Mark 10:22-26).

James wrote: "Go to now, *ye* rich men, weep and howl for your miseries that shall come upon *you*. Your riches are corrupted, and your garments are motheaten. Your gold and silver is cankered; and the rust of them shall be a witness against you, and shall eat your flesh as it were fire. Ye have heaped treasure together for the last days" (Jas. 5:1-3). Paul also wrote to Timothy: "But they that will be rich fall into temptation and a snare, and *into* many foolish and hurtful lusts, which drown men in destruction and perdition. For the love of money is the root of all evil: which while some coveted

8

after, they have erred from the faith, and pierced themselves through with many sorrows. But thou, O man of God, flee these things; and follow after righteousness, godliness, faith, love, patience, meekness" (1Tim. 6:9-11). Does this mean that it is actually impossible for the rich and the wealthy to make heaven?

For the purpose of clarity, the Bible never said money is evil, but the love of it is *the root* of all evil. Jesus rightly said it is they that *trust* in riches, rather than trusting in the God who gives the riches! The *love of* and the *trust in* what we have or posses is the root of all evil and the route to all evil. If we would kill, depose and dethrone the love and affection to our property, possession, riches, wealth, achievements, etc in our hearts, they become servants to obey us, not masters to control us, only then can we follow Jesus.

"Know ye not, that to whom ye yield yourselves servants to obey, his servants ye are to whom ye obey; whether of sin unto death, or of obedience unto righteousness?" (Rom. 6:16). If we will not put our trust in our riches or possession and know that there is nothing we have that is not given by God and if He gave us, He can ask us to give it back to Him, then following Jesus will not be difficult. Paul warned Timothy to "charge them that are rich in this world, that they be not highminded, nor trust in uncertain riches, but in the living God, who giveth us richly all things to enjoy" (1Tim. 6:17).

4
THE EXTRA MILE

"There was a man named Zacchaeus, which was the chief among the publicans, and he was rich. And he sought to see Jesus who he was; and could not for the press, because he was little of stature. And he ran before, and climbed up into a sycomore tree to see him: for he was to pass that way. (Luke 19:2-4)

What extent would many go to see Jesus! What an effort for this man to find Jesus! While the rich and young ruler had the opportunity to see and personally come to Jesus unhindered, Zacchaeus, also a rich and noble man, but disadvantaged in stature could not readily find his way to Jesus, even though he strongly desired to. Out of desperation, he climbed a tree to see Jesus and his desperation finally paid up: Jesus found him on that tree. He saw his sincerity and frantic effort to see him and he gave him audience.

For a rich man like Zachaeaus to climb a tree to see Jesus was a sincere commitment and desire. Jesus saw beyond his deficiency, He saw his heart, just like He saw beyond the good works of the rich young ruler. "For *the LORD seeth* not as man seeth; for man looketh on the outward appearance, but the LORD looketh on the heart" (1Sam.17:7). He scanned him just as he did the young ruler to see what was missing in his life and he found it: "Zacchaeus, make haste, and come down; for to day I must abide at thy house" (Luke 9:5).

We may not know the implication of this statement or this request of Jesus to Zacchaues simply because the man obeyed, but it is no less a request to what Jesus asked the young ruler and he couldn't obey. What Jesus may be asking from individual may differ, He alone knows why He is asking what He is asking. It is not about what He is asking from us, it is the obedience to doing it that matters. Obedience is the greatest virtue of a believer. If we cannot obey, all our sacrifices and activities are in vain and we cannot follow Him.

These two men had something in common: they were both rich and desired to see Jesus and they both saw Him. But the difference in them is while the rich and young ruler could not do what Jesus asked him to do, Zacchaeus was willing; he was ready to give up his possessions to the poor, and restitute all money, wealth, possessions and riches he had gotten illegally four fold, even without being asked to. "Zacchaeus stood, and said unto the Lord; Behold, Lord, the half of my goods I give to the poor; and if I have taken any thing from any man by false accusation, I restore *him* fourfold" (Luke 19:8). He truly met the Lord, didn't he? What a great difference!

We might want to conclude that it appeared as if what Jesus asked from Zacchaeus seemed a lot easier to do than what He asked from the other man. But it is not about what Jesus is asking from us, it is our attachment to it and the obedience in doing it. If He asked for something far less in value and quality, but if we are too much attached to it, it will be as difficult to let go as when He asks for the whole world.

Watch where your treasures are laid up because that is where your heart will also be. If your treasures are laid up in heaven, your affection will be in heaven, so nothing will be difficult for you to give up on earth. Our affection may be on vanity, though, it is vanity, we will not be able to let go anyway, just as much as someone, whose affections is laid on gold and silver. It is the mindset. The whole world with all its treasure is vanity, let alone worthless things like habits, friendship, association or other things. These things should not be big enough to take us to hell. If we possess them, we must dispossess of them.

5
FILTHY RAGS

"But we are all as an unclean thing, and all our righteousnesses are as filthy rags; and we all do fade as a leaf; and our iniquities, like the wind, have taken us away" (Isa.64:6)

Although it is apparent that Zacchaeus was a dubious man who got his wealth illegally and didn't seem to be a religious person. He did not claim to have kept the laws, but rather considered himself a sinner needing restitution. He even lacked societal respect and acceptance of his own people, because they all knew who he was and how he got his money.

The young ruler, however seemed to be a very pious man: got his wealth through legal means and claimed to have kept "all the laws" from his youth, which suggest that he was perhaps a Pharisee, the only religious sect who could boast to have kept all the laws! So, he was a deeply religious person with an enviable position in the society as a ruler. He also loved the Lord!

The achievement of the rich young ruler contributed to his inability to follow Jesus. He came to Jesus with impeccable degrees, qualifications, good works and a religious mindset of a righteous man (according to the law), but the other man came as a sinner, unworthy to even receive Jesus into His house!

When we have qualifications and achievements: like strict adherence to laws, doctrines, church membership, being a worker in the church, Sunday school teacher or laboring in the ministry to win souls for Christ, which things are good, but when they become our certificates and testimonials before the Lord, it will be as difficult to follow Jesus just like this man. It puts us in a performance level rather than relationship with Jesus. The best of our righteousness is filthy rags before God. It's not about what we do, no matter how good and sacrificial, they are nothing to Him: it's about what He did. We must lay down our achievements at the foot of the cross and come just as we are. The only thing we were born with is sin and it's the only qualification to earn salvation. Only sinner needs salvation.

Jesus did not come for the righteous, He came for sinners. "They that are whole have no need of the physician, but they that are sick: I came not to call the righteous, but sinners to repentance" (Mark 2:17). "He giveth power to the faint; and to *them that have* no might he increaseth strength" (Isa.40:29). Whatever we can do by ourselves, we do not need Him for it. If we can be holy through the law, if we can win souls, if we can preach, pray, etc, we do not need Him, because "in him we live, and move, and have our being" (Acts 17:28) and without Him we can do nothing (Jn.15:5).

Let us lay aside all good works, great efforts, religious activities and credentials that may give us a sense of 'working for the Lord'. The world, the society and the religious environment may give us credit, but it may be a stumbling block to Jesus. Jesus admonished us: "So likewise ye, when ye shall have done all those things which are commanded you, say, We are unprofitable servants: we have done that which was our duty to do" (Luke 17:10). Paul said: "But I keep under my body, and bring *it* into subjection: lest that by any means, when I have preached to others, I myself should be a castaway" (1Cor.9:27).

If all our good works are filthy rags to him, we should then come with our hands raised up and not with our hands in our pockets. That is the only acceptable way Jesus can come into our lives and that was why he came to Zacchaeus' life but couldn't' make it to the young ruler's.

6
MAINTAINING THE STANDARD

"Nevertheless the foundation of God standeth sure, having this seal, The Lord knoweth them that are his. And, Let every one that nameth the name of Christ depart from iniquity" (2Tim.2:19).

If we do not come with sin, there is no place for grace, for it is where sin abounds that grace abounds much more (Rom.5:20). If there is no sin in our lives, then there is nothing for the blood of Jesus to cleanse (1Jn.1:7b). If you were never lost, you can never be found. If you were never damned, there is no need to be saved. If you were never sick, you do not need to be healed.

"They that are whole have no need of the physician, but they that are sick: I came not to call the righteous, but sinners to repentance" (Mark2:17). We must lay our greatest achievement down at the feet of Jesus. They must come to the place of ruin. We must say like

Paul: "I count all things *but* loss for the excellency of the knowledge of Christ Jesus my Lord: for whom I have suffered the loss of all things, and do count them *but* dung, that I may win Christ" (Php.3:8).

It is interesting to know that Jesus did not tell the rich young ruler to bring his possessions to Him or to come lay it down at His feet. He did not ask him to bring the proceeds of the sale of his properties to Him to assist His ministry. The fact is that Jesus did not need them just as the man did not need them. Those things belonged to the poor in the physical, not the poor in the spirit. It is the poor in the spirit that shall see God. "Blessed *are* the pure in heart: for they shall see God" (Mat.5:8).

Jesus said: "For after all these things do the Gentiles seek" (Mat.6:32). We are not to seek for them but receive them as gift from Jesus after we receive Him. This man came to Jesus with excess weight of everything he didn't need, but still unwilling to let go. He is a perfect example of many believers today. We must not come to Jesus with offerings in our hands, but rather present ourselves as the offering, a living sacrifice which He will accept (Rom.12:1) and we must come just the way we are. He does not need our things, activities, labour or achievements, He needs us. We must come with our sins and not our good works or efforts which are filthy rags to Him.

Another shocking revelation here is that, in His usual characteristic, Jesus did not call this man back! He did not dress or placate the matter in order to accommodate him. He did not lower the standard, he did not even encourage him to try and not give up so easily. He did not explain anything to him or try to convince him not to perish. He did not tell him the implication of his action and He did not even care if he was losing a potential sponsor of His ministry.

Why didn't Jesus appeal to the emotions of this man as we see today in many sermons where people are begged to accept Christ? Jesus simply spoke the truth and left people to deal with it. 'Good wine need no bush', goes the saying. We do not need to spell out the advantages and benefits of coming to Christ to people. That is the good news of man, but not the Gospel of Christ. The Gospel is to preach Jesus, the truth and leave them with the truth. "Think not that I am come to send peace on earth: I came not to send peace, but a sword" (Mat.10:34).

When we read the following verses, it challenges many preaching and sermon today where benefits of coming to Jesus are always on emphasis to the point of making it so robustly juicy.

"Think not that I am come to send peace on earth: I came not to send peace, but a sword. For I am come to set a man at variance against his father, and the daughter against her mother, and the daughter in law against her mother in law. And a man's foes *shall be* they of his own household. He that loveth father or mother more than me is not worthy of me: and he that loveth son or daughter more than me is not worthy of me. And he that taketh not his cross, and followeth after me, is not worthy of me. He that findeth his life shall lose it: and he that loseth his life for my sake shall find it" (Mat 10:34-39).

What Jesus stated didn't look too attractive to bring people to Him, but prepared their hearts for the decision they were about to make, which is better.

Even when Jesus had the opportunity to convince Pilate during His trials, He did not say anything to the chagrin of the man who had power to set Him free. It was then He spoke: "Thou couldest have no power *at all* against me, except it were given thee from above: therefore he that delivered me unto thee hath the greater sin" (John 19:11).

As believers, we must separate emotions from spirituality. God is not an emotional God, He is a spiritual God, He watches over His words to perform it, not over our emotions. God is Spirit and so are we. We cannot use soul to relate with God. We must not rationalize or think for God or try to help Him like Saul and Uzzah did. He does not need our ability, but availability. He is an all-sufficient God. He has a standard and will not lower His standard because of our ignorance. He will not replace truth with facts in order not to injure our sensibility.

In the book of Revelation, Jesus said: "He that is unjust, let him be unjust still: and he which is filthy, let him be filthy still: and he that is righteous, let him be righteous still: and he that is holy, let him be holy still" (Rev.22:11). He didn't beg them to change. He told Judas: "That thou doest, do quickly" (Jn.13:27). He didn't beg him to stop. He will not compromise His standard. He will not accept your Ishmael, He is asking you for your Isaac.

7
DAMNING THE CONSEQUENCE

"he made haste, and came down, and received him joyfully" (Lk.19:6).

Jesus asking Zacchaeus to lead Him to his house looked like something we would gladly do if we were in his position, but it is the simplest request Jesus has been asking millions of people today that they have not been able to grant. He says: "Behold, I stand at the door, and knock: if any man hear my voice, and open the door, I will come in to him, and will sup with him, and he with me" (Rev.3:20).

For Zacchaeus to take Jesus to his house was a political suicide. Meddling with anything pertaining to religion which was the exclusive preserve of the Priests was politically dangerous to his position as the Chief Customs Officer for the nation. It could lead to such blackmail the priest wanted to unleash on Pilate when he didn't want to convict Jesus. "From thenceforth Pilate sought to release him: but the Jews cried out, saying, If thou let this man go, thou art not Caesar's friend: whosoever maketh himself a king speaketh against Caesar. When Pilate therefore heard that saying, he brought Jesus forth, and sat down in the judgment seat in a place that is called the Pavement, but in the Hebrew, Gabbatha" (Joh 19:12-13)

Zacchaeus' action could lead to the full wrath of the Jews who knew he was a publican, a tax-collector, a position the Jews considered the height of unpatriotism and anti-Jewish; stifling and milking them on tax and remitting it to the Roman Government who had enslaved them. The more he did that, the more commission he got and he had a lot and they knew how. He could be stoned, an act the Jews were expert in. So, they knew him so well and many would swear that if salvation would come to anyone, not Zacchaeus! So, both Zacchaeus and Jesus were in a very great fix and courting a very great consequence: Zacchaeus losing his life, job and status; Jesus losing a crowd of people who could have believed and become His followers!

Believers and leaders today would have seen that as opportunity to make altar call where they can boast of souls coming to Christ in a crusade.

The crowd was huge and that was a very beautiful opportunity for Jesus' ministry to expand, have more disciples, followers and prove to the public that He was truly the Messiah.

Would He jeopardize His ministry because of a man everyone knew was a sinner? But Jesus was not concerned about crowd coming to Him, but about a sinner coming to Him. He said: "I say unto that likewise joy shall be in heaven over one sinner that repenteth, more than over ninety and nine just persons, which need no repentance" (Luke 15:7).

As if talking to [sinner] Zacchaeus was not enough *sin*, according to Jewish customs and traditions, He also offered to follow him to his house and eat there! "When they (the Jews) saw *it*, they all murmured, saying, That he was gone to be guest with a man that is a sinner" (Luke 19:7). Rather for Jesus to have more crowd to Himself, He chose to have one disciple, a sinner.

After the resurrection, Jesus charged the disciples to go to all the world and make disciples of all nations, not gather crowd or keep them as members. The sheep belong to the Chief Shepherd, not the Shepherd. No one is our member and we are a member of no one. No one died for us, but Christ. We are all members of His body.

8
WHERE SIN ABOUNDS

"where sin abounded, grace did much more abound"
(Rom.5:20).

Great sin invokes great grace! Zacchaeus must have been mystified when Jesus told him he was coming to his house. "Jesus, coming to my house?" he must have been bewildered! He whom is forgiven most, love most.

A [sinner) woman poured a costly alabaster oil of ointment on Jesus' feet and wiped it with her hair. When the disciples raised an eye-brow, Jesus told them to let her alone. She had been forgiven the most, so she appreciated the most. Great forgiveness invokes great giving. (Luke 7:41-43). Same with Zacchaeus. He "stood, and said unto the Lord; Behold, Lord, the half of my goods I give to the poor; and if I have taken any thing from any man by false accusation, I restore *him* fourfold. And Jesus said unto him, This day is salvation come to this house, forsomuch as he also is a son of Abraham. For the Son of man is come to seek and to save that which was lost" (Luke 19:6-10).

This man came to Jesus as a sinner, that was why he could receive forgiveness and then, salvation. But the young ruler came to Jesus as a righteous man who had fulfilled all the laws. There was nothing to forgive. Grace could not work in his life because grace is needed only where there is sin and we are saved by grace, too [through faith].

Zacchaeus was willing to give what he had to the poor without being told because he had received eternal life; those things didn't matter to him again. But, the young ruler could not give his possessions to the poor even when being told, because he did not receive eternal life. What Jesus told the young ruler gave him sorrow and he left Jesus. But what He told Zacchaeus gave him joy enough to receive salvation, bring Jesus to his house and give away his possessions, willingly.

Seeing the action of the young ruler, "Jesus looked around and said to his disciples: "How hardly shall they that have riches enter into the kingdom of God! …how hard is it for them that trust in riches to enter into the kingdom of God! It is easier for a camel to go through the eye of a needle, than for a rich man to enter into the kingdom of God" (Mark 10:23-25). The attachment to riches and trusting in our possessions will prevent us from entering the kingdom of God. Do not go to Jesus with your effort to please Him. Go to Him with your sins and lay at His feet. His blood has not and cannot lose its cleansing power, but there must be something to cleanse.

9
LAYING ALL ON THE ALTAR

"and he left all, rose up, and followed him" (Luk 5:28).

Anything you have or posses, but cannot easily lay down or give up is your own riches, wealth and great possession – a mammon, and mammon won't make heaven, would it? (Mark 6:24; Luke 16:13). So, also whatever you cannot do without. The Bible did not record if Zacchaeus still had his job as a publican or not, but it didn't matter to him again if he lost it; he found Jesus. "The kingdom of heaven is like unto treasure hid in a field; the which when a man hath found, he hideth, and for joy thereof goeth and selleth all that he hath, and buyeth that field" (Mat.13:44).

Jesus will take the priciest, juiciest and the costliest from you, because He gave no less for you! God also gave His only begotten Son. Your wealth and riches can only earn you eternal life, if you are willing to sacrifice it in order for Jesus to have a place in our heart!

If God asks you to give certain of your material possessions today, will you be able to? May be you don't consider yourself having "great possession" in that context, but let's start with your car or career; the only one, that you truly love! That's the exact words God used for Abraham when he asked him to sacrifice 'your son, your only son, whom thou lovest" (Gen.22:2). Or maybe it's your land, house, etc. Those may not be big deal to you, but what about something you really cherish, or your entire savings or even your child!

What if God asks you to give up some particular habits, conclusions, decisions, traditions, association, etc, won't there be enough Bible verses to bail yourself out? Some have claimed that He has asked them to personally give up some worldly things in order to follow Him; like putting on jewelries or certain dresses or even habits.

What has He asked you to give up or you are simply giving up what someone else claims He asked him or her to give up but you yourself don't know what He is personally asking you to give up? Consider removing the logs in your own eyes before removing the specks in other people's eyes (if that is necessary).

Your obedience is in doing what He asks

you and not what He ask others. He will only require from you what He asks you to do (Luke 12:48).

What He asked from the rich ruler was not what he asked from Zacchaeus. What He asked Peter to give up was different from what He asked John or Matthew or any other disciples to give up.

Organized church only encourage people to follow them by adhering to the church or denominational beliefs and doctrines, but many followers never got to a personal relationship and faith walk with Jesus to know what He is asking them to give up in order to follow Him. They thought that following or being a member or even worker in a *church* is following Jesus. Following Jesus (not denomination) requires a personal sacrifice and it is an individual thing, not a group, association, denominational or organizational thing.

10
DENOMINATIONAL CROSS

"My sheep hear my voice, and I know them, and they follow me" (Joh.10:27)

Many denominations or movement don't believe or follow certain doctrines because the leadership don't believe them and so it becomes a taboo to them but a delicacy to others, yet all laying claim to divine revelation. When such member changes denomination, he or she might also have to change doctrines.

The woman at the well tried to convince and prove to Jesus that her own denomination (mountain of Samaria) was the right place to worship God and not in Jerusalem [denomination] mountain. The same denominational spirit is currently ravaging the Christendom today. But Jesus set the record straight: worshipping God is not in any mountain, but in spirit and in truth because: "God is spirit, they that worship Him must worship Him in spirit and in truth' (John 4:23-

24).

You can go to the best mountain (denominations) to worship God, but true worship is personal and it is in spirit and in truth and not in doctrine, music or other traditions.

Anyone coming to Jesus must carry his own cross not someone else's or a denomination's. "Then said Jesus unto his disciples, If any *man* will come after me, let him deny himself, and take up his cross, and follow me" (Mat.16:24). While not neglecting the assembly of the saints for fellowship, everyone must step out of the yoke of denomination and crowd that are thronging at Jesus to meet, know and have a personal encounter and relationship with him. It is what Jesus demands, not what you feel you can give!

He asked the rich and young ruler for ALL his possessions, and he had GREAT possession! He asked Zacchaeus for his status. He asked Peter and some of the disciples for their livelihood as fishermen. He asked Paul for his profession. Wherever your treasure is, there your heart will be also (Mat.6:21). Sometimes we only give up what He ask other people to give up but don't even know what He is asking from us because we do not have a personal relationship with Him. Again, we must reiterate that salvation is a personal thing not a group or denominational thing.

While some may truly desire to give anything up just to please God, but great care must be exercised that it is not mere zeal or religion to take just anything from us and give a false and religious impression or satisfaction: it has to be what He is asking from us, not what He asked someone else or what denomination is asking for!

Whatever we give to God without Him asking for it is a commendable, but it does no good if we are unwilling to give him what he specifically demands from us (Luke 10:30-42). We must be guided by His leading, not by our burden and not just religion or sentiment. There is truly something to give up to follow Jesus. Do you know of anything in your life he is asking you to give up and are you in obedience?

For instance, some still struggle with giving God ten percent of their income as tithe (Mal.3:8). If you default and rob God in that, how would you possibly give all? If you cannot give God material thing, how can you possibly give him your heart? "If therefore ye have not been faithful in the unrighteous mammon, who will commit to your trust the true *riches?* (Luke 16:11).

11
GOOD ADVICE

"no man can serve two masters: for either he will hate the one, and love the other; or else he will hold to the one, and despise the other. Ye cannot serve god and mammon"
(Mat.6:24)

What are your riches, wealth and possessions: things that you would rather die than let go of? Social life, fashion, eating, friendship, material thing, drinking, anger, bitterness, hatred, resentment, cheating, smoking, habit, customs and traditional belief, carry over doctrines and mentality, job, etc. these things are a wealth to you and a great possession and perhaps, He has been asking you to let go these things, but you are still holding on to it, you are no better than the young ruler, who went away sorrowfully with his possessions and wealth intact but with the eternal life lost forever.

Paul asked who shall separate us from the love of Christ? Can you also say that and mean it? "Who shall separate us from the love of

Christ? *shall* tribulation, or distress, or persecution, or famine, or nakedness, or peril, or sword? ... Nay, in all these things we are more than conquerors through him that loved us" (Rom. 8:35,37).

I will close with the advice of Jesus in Mat.18:8 and the words of Apostle Paul in Col. 3:5-6 respectively: "Wherefore if thy hand or thy foot offend thee, cut them off, and cast *them* from thee: it is better for thee to enter into life halt or maimed, rather than having two hands or two feet to be cast into everlasting fire". "Put to death therefore your members which are upon the earth: fornication, uncleanness, passion, evil desire, and covetousness, which is idolatry; for which things' sake cometh the wrath of God upon the sons of disobedience".

Gripped with the reality of this, the disciples said to Jesus: "Lo, we have left all, and have followed thee" (Mark 10:28). The key is leaving ALL, not some. God is not only asking for a part of you, but all of you. Not just your heart, but your life. Not just your ten percent, but your all percent. Discipleship is giving all we are and all we have.

Jesus replied the disciples: "Verily I say unto you, There is no man that hath left house, or brethren, or sisters, or mother, or father, or children, or lands, for my sake, and for the gospel's sake, but he shall receive a hundredfold now in this time, houses, and brethren, and sisters, and mothers, and children, and lands, with persecutions; and in the world to come eternal life". (Mark 10:29-30). That sounds like a better deal. Why hold on to what we can't keep, anyway!

"Except a corn of wheat fall into the ground and die, it abideth alone: but if it die, it bringeth forth much fruit" (John 12:24).

Will you trade your great possession to earn for yourself eternal life or keep it and go to hell? Your greatest possession is your heart. If you can't give him your heart, you can't give him any other thing else. He says: "My son, give me thine heart, and let thine eyes observe my ways" (Pro.23:26). It is easy to know if you have given him your heart: the content of your thought determines the ownership of your heart.

Will you give your heart to Him, painful as it may, or walk away with it to hell? "Wherefore if thy hand or thy foot offend thee, cut them off, and cast *them* from thee: it is better for thee to enter into life halt or maimed, rather than having two hands or two feet to be cast into everlasting fire" (Mat.18:8). Your heart is your greatest possession. The decision is yours."He giveth power to the faint; and to *them that have* no might he increaseth strength" (Isa.40:29).

ABOUT THE AUTHOR

Bola Olu-Jordan is a prophetic and apostolic teacher with a passion for Discipleship. He is actively involved in global missions, especially in the sub-Saharan Africa through CAMP, (CRYOUT Africa Mission Project) and also the publisher of CRYOUT, a quarterly Christian Magazine. He has authored many books among which are What God Forgot To Say, Capsules of Faith and The Mystery of Union in Marriage. He is an international conference speaker and married with children.